English
Kills

English
Kills

Poems by
Monica Wendel

Coal Hill Review
Pittsburgh, Pennsylvania

Author Photo: Chris Dunlap
Cover Photo: Gerald Altman
Cover and text design by Katherine Wintersteen
Titles and text set in Bodoni

Printed on acid-free paper.

Coal Hill Review is an imprint of Autumn House Press, a nonprofit corporation with the mission of publishing and promoting poetry and other fine literature.

Autumn House Press receives state arts funding support through a grant from the Pennsylvania Council on the Arts, a state agency funded by the Commonwealth of Pennsylvania, and the National Endowment for the Arts, a federal agency.

ISBN: 978-1-938769-15-3

Contents

Little Pond

I hadn't expected the land to fight so hard against
the farm—at sunset we slept, and by sunrise
the bugs were eating the kale, rain had split the tomatoes,
deer graced their long necks over the electric fence
to part their mouths around corn.

In the stink of it, the heat, Ellen humming some long-
forgotten pop song, fire ants crawled up my leg
as I knelt in hot sandy soil, planting roots of ginger
two knuckles deep. The ants blistered my thighs.
A little piece of heaven, she said the farm was, and divorced
her husband for it. I knew her husband before I knew her—
bearded, big laughed—together we climbed into dumpsters
to rescue battered apples bound for landfill.
What does it take to nourish love. Or a child,
like the one he wanted and she didn't.
Is a fetus a creature that fights the blood that feeds it
until it emerges from one body into its own?
Like the thunderstorm that uprooted
the spotted beans, their dried-out stalks
heavy with seed pods we would break open,
the soil beneath them charged with
the nitrogen the roots had fixed behind.
Even the tomatoes reminded me of women,
their skin split, pink flesh emerging, scarred.

February 4th Diary

In Berlin I said, look, this city was bombed and separated with walls and put back together and here we are now. We should find the neighborhood in East Berlin where my grandmother lived with a doctor's family, hiding, learning how to give injections, the place where she decided not to go to Moscow and become a doctor, the only choice she regrets—

We walked down a hallway littered with dog shit. We sat in a car, stuck in traffic.

I walked a pack of girls to the theater and as we passed a construction site a woman rode up on a Vespa, offering to sell us coffee, and once we arrived at the theater there was no show, only actors sitting in a white-walled basement snorting cocaine and reading Emily Dickinson

Because I could not stop for Death
He kindly stopped for me

until a girl—who? an actor? one I drove?—cut her forearm open on glass and in the white bathroom I held the wound closed watching blood pour over my fingers, running her arm under cold water to stop it, wondering if I should worry about her blood on my skin or if it would wash off if I could wash it off once it stopped—

Grandmother became a scientist instead. I never saw her lab, only heard of it near the waters of Cold Spring Harbor, she grew corn that glowed in the dark its genes spliced with the genes of fireflies, the ELF tried to burn those crops down, *stop frankenfoods fuck GMOs*. She retired to grow tomatoes in the sandy soil of Lloyd Harbor, brought my father and his brother to the Berlin Wall during the 1960s, said, *the Americans, they saved us.*

English Kills

I've been singing in a dead language
about the sun. The children know
it can come back to life; just ask the Israelis

who made up words they couldn't find
in the Torah—*t-shirt, rainbow.*

But *rainbow* must have been there.
Maybe I'm remembering this wrong.
In my dream I was on a farm

presenting a PowerPoint.
One slide was a picture of a mother

kneeling by her child, the other a backyard
abutting the Newton Creek. In real life one of
its branches is called English Kills.

Don't be alarmed:
Kills was only Dutch for something.

Was it stream. Was it water.
They're all dead now, those first discoverers.
My mother is scared of the tunnels

the Gazans are building but I am scared
of any prison, no matter how large,

and must always take the side against the guards—
my stubborn calling. She told me once
that language is a river, not a fish tank.

You can never capture all the words.

Ferguson, Missouri

I huddled under the highway with my ex-boyfriend's brother
who couldn't remember his son's name—*No? No? No-ed?*
he stuttered, until I couldn't stand it anymore and called out,
Noah. But even then the child did not appear.
The syllables, foreign and large, rested between us.
The only way to safety was to leave behind the twisting ramps
that had sheltered us and make our way to the abandoned bridge
spanning the Harlem River.
                              I woke before we could cross.
Maybe he went on without me, left the world
where fathers lose the names of their sons. No: that was the world
we woke into, and when I scrolled through Facebook
I saw him reporting from Ferguson.
The video started playing without any sound. Straight tie,
wide open eyes. Our nation is unrestful.
I wonder whose child will be next, whose *no, no* I heard.

Wheeling, West Virginia

I cried so much last night
that I was super skinny this morning
and I dreamt that we drove to West Virginia
to climb inside a mountain.
The stairs were steep and I was afraid of falling.
We're in the lentil capital of the nation,
you said. But no lentils grow
that deep underground. In the darkness
of the mountain's hollow inside
I ordered shrimp. Each pink body
curled on the plate like a tendoned larva.
Maybe it wasn't really a shrimp between us.
Maybe it was something we had made.
Now I'm waiting for the subway.
All morning I heard its roar from inside the earth.
It said, *the next train is now arriving*
on the Far Rockaway track, please stand away
from the platform edge.
It said, *there is train traffic ahead of us,*
please be patient. A person can travel
for hours underground
and never leave this city.
Sometimes it feels like the future
will never arrive
and I can hear the chambers of your heart
echoing with laughter.

Farragut, Tennessee

A house with a trapdoor to the roof
and from there, a lake—
this roof is the bridge across it.
And the crater in the lake
is rust-red iron through clear water.
Jamison follows me upstairs,
I recognize him by his beard.

Maybe this is all because yesterday
I took Shamar's son to the museum
to look at the butterflies. The eyes
on their wings looked like dark
holes. Nabokov would have liked it all,
the pinned-up bodies, the children
sticking their arms into the exhibit.
Did anyone think he was yours? Shamar
asked when we met him on the steps.
You could be—you know—

It feels like there are caves inside me
made up of limestone and sandstone
that fill up with water and salt.
The minerals turn milky and drip from the roof.
They tap-tap. They sound like footsteps.

The Evergreens

Last night, in a gray farmhouse,
a girl offered me a drug I'd never
heard of, one with a girl's name,
and I took it after learning how to spell it.
The *A* came before the *E*,
like *Aeneid* or some other ancient story.
My room multiplied into ghosts,
the trash can a man kneeling in the corner,
boneless and small. It's been so long
since I was in another country
that this is the only way to find the new,
like the time I sat on that boy's bed
and sang with his band near the windows
looking out over the graveyard
like we were music and not already gone.

Other Islands

At the wedding, far from the farm, I held the flowers Ellen grew,
trying to see their faces as they promised love. It wasn't easy;
sunshine glared off the warm Gulf waters. Years before,
we were in the park, high on mushrooms, when we heard the news
that Osama bin Laden had died, his body thrown
out of a helicopter into the ocean, no final resting place, no grave
as a gift, and we felt, then, that the blanket we were sitting on
was a very safe place in a world that expanded all the time,
a world ballooning with violence, and we resolved to stay
on our square as long as we could, watching the clouds turn
from one creature into another. She was my next-door neighbor then,
her front stoop overflowing with potted plants that climbed
the fence between her place and mine. Inside, a spider plant
hung under a skylight, spilling into air. When she left New York
her love followed her, and they wed and divorced all in short time.
What do any of us know, when we talk about love?
We needed each other as bin Laden's limbs dropped
from the sky into a deep blue sea. In the sun I saw
the eyes of soldiers flecked with gold, their bodies
carapaced. I felt poisoned the next day. And he was still dead.

Back Home

one of my students disappears underground
into the subway, carrying her mother's purse, wearing cream-
colored high heels. She reminds me of Ellen—the black hair,
a wildness that's hard to explain but exists as solidly
as a granite stone flecked with mica, flashes of light and black.
In one picture, hanging in the Laundromat, she's posing
for fifth-grade graduation. In another, she's grainy,
her body a newspaper comic, one hand closing the door
of her apartment building, caught by security camera.
In this city, rivers open their mouths, swallowing each other,
joining, and the harbor says to the rivers, come here,
and the ocean to the harbor says, come here, and the moon pulls
all of the water on earth without saying anything,
just doing, moving its silent way across the sky
which is turning from purple-brown to light blue in morning.
Meanwhile her brother moves the potted plants
from the fire escape to inside—no matter if they die
without sun—and sets up watch in their place.
Wears a red shirt that everyone's eyes rise to,
a bright wing against the faded building. He meets my gaze.
Fourteen, and she eleven. When she comes home,
she won't say where she's gone, is no snitch. She pulls
a baseball cap over her eyes, doodles her own name: *Angel.*

Blue

Billy Joel plays at the diner where the waitresses wear their hair swooped up, swirl whipped cream atop hot cocoa—outside, fall rain shakes the last red leaves from tree branches and rustles ghosts out of sleep—only two months ago cars lined up to wash in the open fire hydrant, little kids with plastic buckets dammed the gutter—last night, I dreamt that Chris and I rowed through New York Harbor at night, as we did the sea expanded until the harbor became a great lake became an ocean—the waitress stirs creamer into coffee, a single revolution of the spoon—puts it in the bus bin—now it's the dishwasher's problem—this rain, will it overflow the system, will sewage drain into the East River—in the bottom silt, divers found the gun used to murder a cop in East Harlem—lights of police boats lined both shores, Bronx and Manhattan—the Narrows, where water whirlpools, sucks boats into ghosts—my father told me how he lent out his hammer to a diver who dropped it near some retaining wall—my father told me that Battery Park shouldn't be there, the land just fill from subway tunnels—in my dream, the wind, cold, blew across the harbor and I found a blanket and curled under it—I woke, cold, curled under a blanket—in the dream, it was others who were rowing, we weren't—from the top deck of the ferry ghosts lit candles on shores that pulled away from us like a canal opening its locks—in our wake, kayakers crossed—the waitress stirs the coffee, again—a new spoon—all this, just once—the dream just once, the rain just once, my father sketching blueprints in the basement— we wrapped Christmas presents in the discarded papers—cities planned and never realized—perfect angles—nothing like these shores—shellfish filter the water, still, sewage spills—I woke just this once—I woke to stir coffee to sit in traffic to watch the river turn red with siren lights with brake lights—I woke to remember my father—the tilt of his drafting board—when we were good we were allowed to do our homework there— borrow his pencils—what city floats through this dream—I am beneath the dock—I swim from one harbor to the next—I burn in sun—I burn tongue—I rake up the shark washed on the sand and bury it—rowers cut across the wake—harbor full of ghosts—whose

Vilnius

In Lithuania
my roommate made art
about hating Jews—

I escaped to a field
where I watched boys play soccer.

Things were dangerous.
I rode the elevator back up to the apartment,
pushed her against the wall
shouting about soldiers
looking for people like me.

She looked surprised
that ideas could have consequences.

I didn't destroy her art.
I woke up instead
and turned off the air conditioner
and took the dog out.
Gray clouds marbled over red brick buildings,
over the old factory we live in.

You were still sleeping.
In darkness, at night, your paintings
become the flags ships use
to signal each other
across wide empty spaces—
this one for civic pride,
this one for genocide.

Better Ones

I can't tell my worst self from my better one. Can you?
Our window faces an alley from which I can never see the moon.
Love, I beg us to move. Finger the ring you put around me and cry
which isn't that strange—I cry almost every day. When you asked
we were on a mountain overlooking the hilly Palouse—pine trees
rooted deep in Idaho's volcanic soil. You said you remembered
when Mount St. Helens erupted, the ashes everywhere—no, you didn't
say that then, you said something kinder, something about us.
You cried while asking. And later I cried and then we ate pizza
before choosing a ring. Picking out an apartment is harder.
I want a two bedroom, for when a baby comes, but that's far off,
or is it, it doesn't have to be, it can be close once we start trying,
but we haven't started yet. Yesterday at work, one of the tiny kids
looped one arm around my neck, leaned her sticky bangs
against my chest, and let her whole weight fall, until she slept.

Magadan, Russia

The tide moved out, then
froze, foam becoming white veins.
The child beside me grew up in Siberia,
said, *that was the race, our medals*

waiting there for finishing.
Was he dead? He was.
We sat in the car, looking
at the sea a little longer.

It was unfair that anything
could be so blue. It was unfair
that the grownups made them swim
to their death in the icy waves.

He explained this like I wouldn't
have seen it without his ghost
to guide me. When I woke, the dog
stared up at me from her bed.

The child wasn't quite gone,
he flickered in pre-dawn. So I showered
and had sex and then the cliffs
appeared even stronger—

limbs of ice, thumbs pressed
against the throat of sky—

if my child is already dead
this was the dream to tell it.

Keep Snowy Waves in Summer

After heavy rains, the tree roots crack the sidewalk open.
It hinges like a door, ravines tracing the outlines of a map
I'm learning how to read. I thought of how a river
deposits sediments, and those sediments change the river's course.
Am I only thinking these things because it's so hard
to find your way underground? Like something has to guide us
in between subway tunnels and sewer lines and the water pipes
and if I could only find that blueprint, spread it out over the roof
and make my way along its hard-edged lines there would be an answer.
Angel came back, for a moment, holding a birthday present
in penitent palms. We asked her to stay, to help puzzle out
a sentence from Latin into English: *In vere flue lenis, et serva nivales*
undas in aestate. But it was no one's birthday, and then her mother
ordered her back home. *College isn't for girls like her,* her mother
told me when I called that evening, begging for Angel's return.
I felt a door close in my heart. Then I felt it open again.
The rains here water even dead languages. They find soil
where it seems like there was none, and roots grow.

Paris

The summer ends. I say good-bye to the camp kids,
their Latin workbooks, their parents holding phones set
to record them singing *tu es sol meus, my only sunshine.*
You come on the last day, the trip-to-the-beach day,
and we stand holding hands, a border for tag, near
the waters of Jamaica Bay. Our city's skyline floats
12, 13 miles off. On the subway home you sketch
fish scales, hammerhead sharks, Moby Dick rising
from the ocean. One city sinks and another endures.
The world continues to roll over, turning toward
the sun, and terrorists strike Paris. I think that my body
is a gift. And language another gift. And land, too,
can be a gift, the kind of gift that emerges when refugees
float across narrow seas to reach safe banks. We want
a refuge. We want a family that can swim together.
We want life vests and a cell phone kept dry
in a ziplock bag. I don't know what it's like
to flee from one world to the next, but I expect that—
like dream—one can call back. Text and say,
are you there. Paris, who caused the Trojan war,
when you sail between these Greek islands, propelled
by Helen's beauty, the whims of the gods, do you
shudder as the motors of inflatable rafts are dropped
into water? What rivers do we cross to find each other?
To find our children? To find our way home?

Acknowledgments

Grateful acknowledgment is made to the following publications in which the poems first appeared:

7 x 7	"Little Pond," "Back Home," "Better Ones," "Keep Snowy Waves in Summer," "Other Islands," "Paris"
Burrow Press Review	"February 4th Diary," "Wheeling, West Viriginia"
Day One	"The Evergreens" (under the title "Wilson Avenue")
Forklift, Ohio	"Magadan, Russia"
Gandy Dancer	"English Kills," "Vilnius"
Paper Nautilus	"Farragut, Tennessee" (Nominated for a Pushcart Prize, 2014)

Thanks is due to Diana Delgado and Emily Hockaday for reading this manuscript at various stages and to Jackie Sherbow for her feedback on individual poems. Finally, thanks is due to Paulin Paris, whose generous collaboration helped create the poems in *7x7*.

About the Author

Monica Wendel is a Brooklyn-based poet and educator. She studied philosophy at Johns Hopkins University and the State University of New York at Geneseo and received her MFA in poetry writing from New York University, where she was awarded Goldwater and Starworks teaching fellowships. She is the author of *No Apocalypse*, a full-length collection that won the Georgetown Review Press poetry manuscript contest, and the chapbooks *Call it a Window* (Midwest Writing Center, 2012) and *Pioneer* (Thrush Press, 2014). Her poems have appeared in the *Bellevue Literary Review*, *Ploughshares*, *Rattle*, and other journals. A former writer-in-residence at the Jack Kerouac Project of Orlando, Florida, she is now a writing mentor at Still Waters in a Storm and assistant professor of composition and creative writing at St. Thomas Aquinas College.

The *Coal Hill Review*
Chapbook Series